To my paren

...who reluctantly came
computers can be useful!

Whatever your reasons for learning how to use a computer, you don't want, or need it to be hard, complicated or stressful. This guide makes learning computer basics easy and fun. Really!

www.myparentsfirst.com

Live, Love, Learn

The sale of this book, and other books published by KLMK Enterprises, help raise funds for cancer research. Find a cure.

Published by KLMK Enterprises, www.myparentsfirst.com

Printed by Hignell Printing in Winnipeg, MB, Canada
Third Edition, August 2008. Reprinted July 2010

ISBN 978-0-9732728-4-0

Hi, I'm Louise. Don't worry, if you think computers are NOT user friendly and about as foreign as Mars, you're not alone!

The fact is, that computers are getting harder to avoid. It's to the point that people just assume you have e-mail or can "check it out on the website."

Whatever your reasons for learning how to use a computer, you don't want or need it to be hard, complicated or stressful.

With the help of this little guide, thousands have learned the simple basics in no time at all. You can too.

My Parents First Computer and Internet Guide makes learning how to use a personal computer easy and fun. - *Really!*

And YES, this book includes instructions for both Windows XP and Vista!

I've always felt that the easiest way to learn is by doing...So let's get going!

Easy as 1, 2, 3...

This easy guide is set up in three steps.

The first step, *What's what,* will get you familiar with the different parts of your computer. The second step, *Ready, Set, Go,* will teach you how to use your computer. And, the third step *the Internet and E-mail* will get you onto the World Wide Web (www)!

There are even Bright Idea pages, set aside just for you, to jot down your own notes!

Keep this guide by your computer for easy reference.

Step 1 *What's what*

There are a lot of pieces to a computer and they can be confusing. In the next few pages you will see what's what!

The Parts

How & where to set it up

The Mouse

The Keyboard

What's what...the parts

A Computer System
All the parts together, are your computer system.

The Tower
The tower is essentially the *computer*. It holds the main computer chips that are the brains of your computer system. If you are asked by a technician to "bring in your computer", the tower is usually the only part they want!

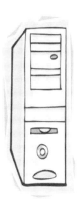

What's what...the parts

Inside and outside of the tower are different *drives,* where information is stored or retrieved. The main drive in your computer, where the most information is, is the *C drive.*

The **C drive** is inside your computer.

On the outside of your computer you will see other types of drives:

- **CD Drive**: New games or programs generally come on a Compact Disk (CD) and you need a CD drive to load them into your system. There will be a button close to the drive to make it open. CD's are placed in label side up.

- **CD Burner:** If you want to create your own music CD or store photos on a CD, then you will need a CD burner.

- **Floppy Disk Drive**: In older computers you might also see a floppy disk drive, newer models don't include them. Before CDs floppies were the thing.

What's what...the parts

All the parts of your computer system will connect to the tower. The printer, the monitor, speakers, a mouse – everything, all need the computer to tell them what to do.

Laptop computers don't have a tower; their brains are all tucked in under the keyboard or behind the monitor. Talk about Mighty Mouse technology!

What's what...the parts

The Monitor

A *monitor* is the most important part that is attached to your computer, after all without it you can't see what is going on! The monitor is a window between you and your computer and the **W**orld **W**ide **W**eb (www).

Most monitors have some dials on them and just like a TV, these are to adjust the brightness or to move the picture side to side, or up or down. You most likely won't have to make any adjustments with these dials, but if someday you come to your screen and it's all wonky or worse, dark, don't panic! Someone has fiddled with them, and you just have to fiddle them back again.

What's what...the parts

The Printer
You might choose a color printer or one that only uses black ink. Having color is pretty cool, but color ink can be expensive. Check out how much the replacement cartridges are!

Every printer is different in the way that you have to load the ink. Some are easier than others. Some warranties are void if you do not use their own brand of ink to refill them.

There are two types of printers, *inkjet* and *laser.* An inkjet printer is less expensive, and the most common for home computers. A lot of offices use laser printers.

Be sure to ask the sales clerk lots of questions about the printer and, when you get it home, read your printer manual for details.

The Speakers
Sometimes speakers will be built in, but more often than not, they're separate. With speakers you can listen to music or a video. Maybe one day you'll be really high tech and enjoy a video phone call! How cool would that be!

Now, to put it all together!...

What's what... how & where

Cables, Plugs and Stuff

The printer, speakers, monitor and anything else
you have with your system are all connected to your
computer with *cables.*

Plugging it all in might seem a little daunting when you
first look at it. It's NOT! If you know how to put a round
peg into a round hole, and a square peg into a square
hole, you can hook up your computer! REALLY!

Ports

Port, is just the computer world's word for outlet.
Ports are where you plug your cables into. You will
find many ports in the back of a computer, in many
different shapes and sizes! This is where it gets easy.

A *port* is connected to a *card* or *component* inside
your computer. For example, you will see a port for
your speakers, another for your printer, another for
the monitor, etc.
If you have more accessories, you need to
have more *ports!*

What's what... how & where

What Plugs into What
This is where the computer world went right. Each piece of equipment has a different shaped plug and will ONLY fit into its specific port! Some of them are the same, such as the mouse and keyboard ports, so it doesn't matter which port you choose!

Something special, USB Ports
Universal Serial Bus, or USB's are great! Things like a digital camera, a webcam, a joystick for flight simulator, need a USB port to connect to a computer.

Accessories like these often feature "Plug and Play", a very cool thing that makes *loading a program* and hooking up a device simple as pie. USB ports are a bit like a highway interchange, offering accessories a quick and easy connection to your computer.

Screws
Some of the plugs have screws on each side of them. This is just to ensure that the cable doesn't get jostled out accidentally and to make sure you have it plugged in all the way. Tighten them up, but not as tight as a lug-nut!

What's what... how & where

Where should you set up?
Set your computer up in a comfortable area where it won't get in the way. Once you are all hooked up, you won't want to move it anywhere. Having a desk is nice, but even the kitchen table will do.

Where to avoid setting up
Do not set up your computer next to a microwave or close to any magnets. Magnets have the capability to *STRIP* data from computer disks and electronics. Stay away from moist areas too -- electronics do not like to be wet!

Power Source
You will need to dedicate a power outlet in your home to your new computer. I suggest you get a power bar with a *surge absorber* to plug all your computer parts into.

If your home suffered a power surge, (maybe a lightening strike?) without surge protection your computer would get fried! I have one with 6 outlets on it and am surprised that they are all filled up!

What's what... the mouse

A new mouse in your house!

The Mouse
The invention of the computer mouse has made it possible for even the most technology-frightened person to feel like a pro. Basically, it's a simple extension to your keyboard.

The Mouse Pad
When your system is all set up, the mouse will be to one side of your keyboard, on a mouse pad. The pad is not essential, but will prolong the life of your mouse. Besides, it's nice to have something soft to rest your wrist on!

On Your Monitor
An arrow, or the cursor, will move around on your screen when you move your mouse. They will move together. Your Cursor will follow your Mouse anywhere, like a good dance partner!

Left-click, Right-click
The top of your mouse has two buttons. To *right-click,* simply press down on the right button. To *left-click,* press down on the left button.

What's what... the mouse

The Left-click
If you move the mouse around your screen and left-click, your *cursor* will instantly arrive at that spot! The left-click is used for <u>giving commands.</u>

The Double-click!
This is an important little thing to know how to do. You'll hear many times to double-click on something to open it. Double-clicking is always done with the left-click.

The best way I can describe it is by thinking of music beats. You know the song "Happy Birthday?" You sing the word "happy" in one beat. To get a double-click beat, sing "happy" twice in the same amount of time that you would normally sing it once. TA DA!

The Right-click
The right-click is used for <u>getting commands</u> This will all make sense when we practice, further along in the book.

A Mouse Roller
A computer mouse might also have a *roller*. Try it out, with it you can easily scroll up and down pages on your computer.

Bright Ideas

➢

➢

➢

➢

➢

➢

➢

What's what...the Keyboard

The keyboard is your typewriter. You will find all the regular keys that have always been on a typewriter, and a few extras.

Not all keyboards are the same. Here is a more traditional design:

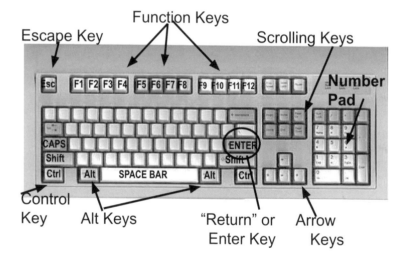

Function Keys

Escape Key

Scrolling Keys

Number Pad

Control Key   Alt Keys   "Return" or Enter Key   Arrow Keys

The keys can be very diverse. In different programs the keys can even be used for different things, often offering shortcuts to commands.

On the next few pages we'll learn about the extra keys. The keys other than the letters! We'll start with the key on the top left-hand corner, the Esc key and work our way around clockwise.

What's what...the keys

Esc Key

Esc is short for *Escape*. It can be used to close, cancel or escape from the most current thing you are doing on your computer.

Function Keys: F1 to F12

The Function Keys offer different shortcuts with different programs. In fact, with the help of the *"F"* keys, you can do almost anything you ask your mouse to do!

Let me tell you something about myself. I've been using a computer for 20 years or so and I would be the first to say that the function keys are great. Then I would be the first to ask, "So, how do I use them?"

My opinion? That for average computer users, the function keys are mostly there to collect dust!

What's what...the keys

Print Screen/Sys RQ, Scroll lock
and Pause/Break

I don't mean to disappoint you, but the next three keys are used even less than the function keys! Unless you get into programming, you will most likely never use them. Although, I have enjoyed a fun little trick *Print Screen* can do.

When you press the Alt & Print Screen keys together you can capture a snapshot of your computer screen that you can paste onto another document!

You may never need or want to do that, but what the heck, I thought I'd mention it anyway!

Next, in *Ready, Set, Go!*, when we learn about editing, I'll show you how to *paste* a picture onto a document!

What's what...the keys

The Number Pad

The *number pad* is on the very right hand side of most keyboards. There is a key marked *Num* or *Num Lock* on the top left corner of it. Press it once and it is turned on, press it again and it is turned off. There is a little light close by to indicate if it is on or not.

When ON, the number pad will work like a calculator. When OFF it works like the arrow and scrolling keys. Have a look at #4 – it also has an arrow on it pointing left, #6 has an arrow point right.

Number Lock Key

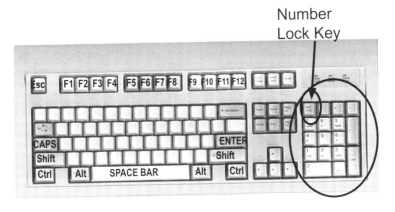

Remember, never let your computer get you too frustrated... *I don't know how many times I have caught myself thinking that the ruddy thing is broken, only to find out (eventually) that the function I want is not turned on...*

What's what...the keys

Arrow Keys
Much like your mouse, the *arrow keys* move the *cursor** around on your screen. Left, right, up or down.

The arrow keys can also help you scroll through a web site. Press the down arrow to move down the page, or press the up arrow to move up the page!

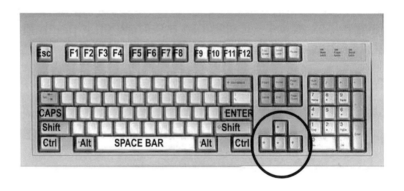

*Cursor: A blinking line on your computer screen that tells you where your mouse is active or, where you would type if you were typing.

not a curser...

What's what...the keys

Crtl Key
Ctrl is short for *Control* and is used together with other keys for many commands in different programs. For instance, if you want your letter to be double spaced, press *Crtl + the number 2 together*.

Shift Key
The *shift key* will change lower case letters into capital letters. If you look across the keyboard you will see another key with a similar arrow on it. That is a shift key for your other hand!

Enter Key
Often, when you give your computer a command, you will hit the *Enter* key to finalize it. The *enter* key is also the *return* key, when you are using your keyboard like a typewriter!

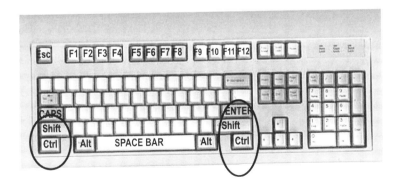

What's what...the keys_

Backspace/Erase Key
The Backspace/Erase key, on the main part of the keyboard in the top right corner, will back up and erase whatever is behind the cursor.

Scrolling Keys
This group of six keys is used for *scrolling* through documents or web sites.

I'll explain the top three keys, right to left and then we'll go over the bottom row.

Once we open a program or get onto a web page you will see how easy and helpful these keys really are!

What's what...the keys

Scrolling, top row

- **Insert:** Activate this key and when you type, your typing will go right OVER what's there, erasing your original work as you go. OR, push it again and your typing will stay in *front* of your original work, pushing previous work along. *I have a love/hate relationship with this key.*
- **Home:** This key will bring you back to the beginning of the *line* you are on or, press *Crtl + Home* together and your cursor will go to the beginning of the document you are viewing. The start of a page or document is usually referred to as "Home."
- **Page Up:** will automatically scroll one page up.

Insert	Home	Page Up
Delete	End	Page Down

Scrolling, bottom row

- **Delete:** Press *the Delete* key to erase what is just ahead of your cursor.
- **End:** Press the *End* key and your cursor will jump to the end of the line you are working on, or; press *Crtl + End* together and your cursor will go to the end of your document!
- **Page Down:** Press the *Page Down* key and you will automatically scroll your screen down to the next page.

What's what...the keys

Alt Key
Simply put, the *Alt* key *alters* the capability of other keys. Almost every program can use the Alt key, but the command combinations are very often different. I think of the Alt key as a little more *high brow* so to speak, it's always used for things that are more complicated than a straight forward command.

Space Bar
The Space Bar works the same as it does with a typewriter. Press it and you will move the cursor along one space. Very handy for leaving spaces between words!

Caps Lock and Shift Keys
When you press the Caps Lock key you lock the letters to type in CAPITALS. Press it again and you will un-lock them and type in lower case again.

Press the Shift key with a letter and it will Capitalize it. The Shift key also lets you type the symbols above the numbers!

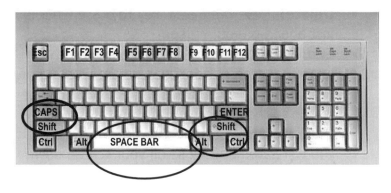

Step 2

Step 2

Step 2 *Ready, Set, Go!*

On the next few pages we will get you turned on, opening a program and using it. We'll do it step-by-step, so let's get going!

The Menu Bar

Let's Turn You On

The On Button

Most new computers have the *On* button easily accessible on the front of the tower.

Push it and your computer will begin to turn itself on. Turning itself on might take a minute or so. When your computer starts, it also starts a few *programs* that it will use while it's on.

TIP #1 If a window pops up asking for a password, just click on the *Enter* button, otherwise you will have to use that password every time you turn on!

TIP #2! If at start-up your computer freezes on a black and white screen with this message near the bottom, **"Non-system disk or disk error."** DON'T WORRY! If you have a computer with a floppy disk drive, check it and take out the floppy disk. Windows won't start with a floppy disk inserted.

Let's Turn You On

The Re-Set Button
Re-Set, Re-Boot, Re-Start. These are all different names for the same thing. You will generally find this button located near the On button. Not all computers have this button.

What's the Re-Set Button for?
As a beginner (or as an expert for that matter) you may overload or confuse your computer into freezing itself into a state of total non-compliance. When this happens, press the Re-Set button and your computer will Re-Start. It will go through all the regular start-up stuff and maybe do a little self-maintenance as it re-boots itself.

Is Re-booting safe to do?
If your computer freezes while you have been working on a document, you might need to re-boot. It is safe, but all the work you did from the last time you saved it, will be lost ☹. Unfortunately, it is usually the best (and often only) way to get things going again.

> TIP: If your computer does not have a re-set button, there is a *keyboard combination* that you can use to re-boot.
> **Press the *"Crtl + Alt + Delete"* keys together** and follow the on-screen instructions.

Vista

Vista is the newest Operating System released by Microsoft. Most new personal computers will come with it installed. The last big release was Windows XP.

Operating systems set the look and feel to your computer. All the programs in your computer must be compatable and work with the Operating System.

Using Vista feels like when I got a new couch for the living room. Updated, nice and new, but - *thank heavens* - it's still a couch!

With that said, you will see a few pages here and there that should help you with the few differences between XP and Vista.

Start Menu

Where?

You will find the word *Start* on a button in the lower left-hand corner of your screen. Click on *Start* to open the *Start Menu*. The bar that it is sitting on is called the *task bar*.

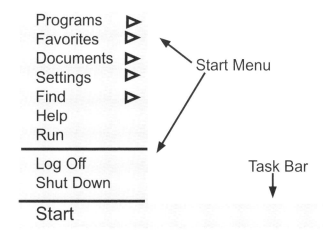

What does the Start button do?

The Start button works as a door into your computer. Move your mouse over the Start button, left-click and the Start menu will pop up. Each item on this menu can be referred to as a *program*, a *folder* or a *file*.

You could think of the start button as a drawer in a filing cabinet, open it to see what's inside!

If the folder has an arrow beside it, that means there's more to see.

It is as simple as it sounds!

Start Menu

Shut Down
The best way to turn off your computer is through the *Start menu*.

Click on the Start button and slide your mouse up to "shut down" and left-click.

A window similar to this one will pop up, click on the option you want!

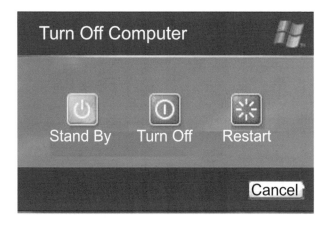

Stand By will power down your computer if you will be away from it for a while. Great for saving energy!

If your computer gets turned off some other way (maybe a power outage), you will see a maintenance program automatically run when you re-start it.

Vista - Start Menu

Internet Internet Explorer	Owner Documents Pictures	
E-mail Windows Mail	Music Games	
Backup/Restore Microsoft Word Microsoft Excel Windows Update Media Player	Search Recent Items Computer Network Connect to	Switch User Log Off Lock
All Programs ➜	Control Panel Default Programs Help & Support	Restart Sleep Hibernate
Start Search		Shutdown

With Vista, you will no longer see the "Start" button. Instead, you will click on the Windows Logo® to open up the Start menu.

The Start menu has mostly the same features as Windows XP, just rearranged a bit. Notice the list above "All Programs", this will keep changing to feature the last programs you used! I like it!

Start Menu

Settings
The Settings folder contains the key programs that help to fine tune your computer.

It is the path to the **_Control Panel,_** where you will find tools to personalize and organize your computer.

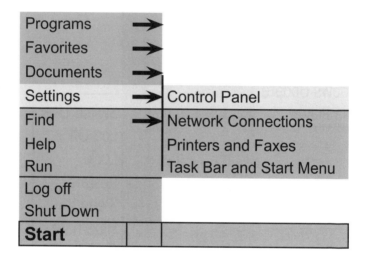

- *Network Connections* is used to connect your computer to another computer.

- *Printers and Faxes* holds the tools to connect and install your printer.

- *Task Bar and Start Menu* lets you personalize your desktop, screensaver and the colors on your screen.

Start Menu

Documents file

What a handy file! It keeps documents that you have been working on just one click of the mouse away. Whenever you want, you can go into this file to access the documents you were working on last.

Programs

Move your mouse on top of the word *Programs* and you will see a number of titles pop up beside it. These are folders that contain all the different *programs* installed in your computer. A few of the more popular programs are:

- **Microsoft <u>Word</u>** A word processing program for typing letters and more.

- **Microsoft <u>Excel</u>** A spreadsheet program for accounting, making forms and more.

- **<u>Accessories</u>** This folder has lots of great programs in it, from games to a calculator. There is even a repair kit for your computer to fix itself!

You will see many other programs listed here. Don't be afraid to "point and click"! **The best and easiest way to learn is to explore and try it out.** Computers are really pretty tough, so don't worry about breaking it.

Vista - Sidebar

Vista has this very cool, new feature. It is called a "Sidebar" and the items on it are called "Gadgets".

Here's how to get rid of the Sidebar, change what side it is on, change whether or not you see it all the time, or even alter up the Gadgets...

Right-click on the little icon for it in the right hand side of the task bar. (Along beside where the time is.)

A window will pop up showing its "properties". From here it's easy to change things up.

I like the gadget for the weather. You can change it to reflect almost any city you want!

Common Threads

Here's some really good news for you. Most programs have common threads to each other.

When you learn one, it's easier to learn another!

Once you know the basic commands, you will find it easy using those commands in other programs.

Since *Microsoft Word* ® is such a great basic program that's simple to learn, we will use it to learn from!

The best way to learn is by doing, so...

LET'S DO SOMETHING!

Open Microsoft Word:

1. Point your mouse over Start, left-click.

2. Slide your mouse up to Programs, then over to Microsoft Word.

3. Left-click and you're in!

Microsoft Word

Now, if you just wanted to type a plain looking letter with the standard factory settings, you're all set. But, if you want to *spice it up*, *Word* makes it easy enough for even the most amateur of us to create something spectacular! Things like:

TYPING IN DIFFERENT colors

type Small or BIG, or *Fancy!*

- You can check your spelling and grammar.
- You can create a table and even alphabetize it!
- Erase mistakes and even undo your erases!
- *Word* can help you format a letter.
- *Word* can help you with your Resume.
- You can even insert pictures!

When you make the leap from paper to computers you will hear some new terms, but really they are just the same old things with new names. For instance:

jotting down the facts = data entry

flipping through the pages = scrolling

creating a letter = word processing

Microsoft Word

Notice that "Microsoft Word" is written in the top left corner of your screen. It is typical for the name of the program (or web site) you are working on, to be located here. This bar is called the **Title Bar** (the blue section).

Title Bar

Name of the Program or Web Site here

File Edit View Insert Format Tools Table Window Help

Menu Bar

Below the *title bar*, you will see a **menu bar** . The menu bar contains commands to run a program. The commands are very common to most programs.

Icons

Under these typical headings, you will often see a row or two of small pictures.

These are called **icons**. *Icons* are shortcuts to some of the more common commands you will use, such as: opening a file, saving, copying, and printing etc.

If you point your mouse over an icon, in a second or two a bubble will appear to tell you what it does.

Microsoft Word

Just before we get on with the Menu Bar, we need to quickly cover the **top three boxes!**

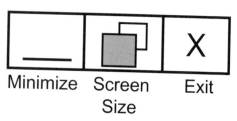

On the top right hand corner of almost any screen, you will see these three boxes in a row.

- **Minimize**
  Left-click on minimize and you will shrink what you have open on your screen **into the Task Bar.** You will see the document's title on a tab in the task bar; to re-open it, all you have to do is click on the tab.

- **Screen Size View**
  Left-click on the middle box to change the size of the window you're viewing.

- **Exit**
  Left-click on the "X" to close the program **or** document you have open. On a good note, most programs will ask if you want to save the changes to the document you are working on before it is COMPLETELY closed and filed away.

Thank you very much!

The Menu Bar

The following pages will teach you how to access and use basic commands from the Menu Bar; from File to Help.

File Edit View Insert Format Tools Table Window Help

Let's get going!

If you haven't got *Word* open, open it now.

Left-click through this path

Start > Programs > Microsoft Word

the File menu

File Edit View Insert Format Tools Table Window Help

New	Ctrl + N
Open	Ctrl + O
Close	
Save	Ctrl + S
Save-As	
Save-As HTML...	
Page Setup	
Print Preview	
Print	
Send to	→ Mail Recipient...
Properties	Routing Recipient...
	Exchange Folder...
1)	
2)	
3)	
4)	
Exit	

Crtl + (a letter)
Is a shortcut you can
use instead of going
through the File menu!

Your last few documents
will show up here. Just click
on the title to open it!

the File menu

New

Plain and simple, this will open up a new document for you. There are two ways to do this, each has its advantages.

A. When you use *New* from the File menu, a window will automatically open up giving you an assortment of choices for what type of new document you might want to open. This is where you can find resume templates too!

Here's how:

1. Move your mouse up to File, left-click

2. Move it down to New, left-click.

3. In the window that pops up, left-click over "Blank Document."

A new blank document might just appear, or if you see an OK button, left-click that too, to open it up!

B. By Left-clicking on the New icon, you will go straight to the plainest blank document possible for the program you are using.

the File menu

Open

This is your gateway to open any **saved** document you have. Open files by going through the *File menu*, or using the *open icon*, which looks like an open file. **Left-click on** *Open* to see a window like this:

Open			
Look in:	Folder Name Here	You will see icons here	
Folder names are listed here. Folders will look either closed or open. If open, you will see the names of the files inside it listed next!	Sometimes you will have a preview window here, showing you a peek of what you have clicked over.	OPEN
		CANCEL
		ADVANCED
File Name		Property		Find Now
Files of Type		Modified		New Search

When a *folder's name* is in the "Look-In" box, the titles of the documents that are filed within that folder are shown, like the files in a filing cabinet!

Here's how to open a document from this window:

1. Left click your mouse over the document title to highlight it, left-click.
2. Double-click on the title to open it.

           or

   Once the title is highlighted, you can left-click on the *Open* button.

File Name, Files of Type, Text or Property or Last Modified, can help you search for a file or document.

the File menu

Close
Close is used to close the document you have open.
Click on *Close* and you will be asked:

"Do you want to save the changes you made to _?"

"Yes, No or Cancel"

Left-click on the option you want.

You can also close a document without closing the program by clicking on this shortcut, found on the top right hand corner of your screen.
Remember the three boxes?

Minimize   Screen   Exit
Size

Both the program AND the open document will
have their own set of these boxes.
Exit the program or just the document...

Open, Close...
No Problem!

the File menu

Save

Like the name suggests, *Save* is for saving whatever document you are working on. Once a document is saved it can be closed and re-opened, changed or edited anytime.

Every time you **save a new document,** you are **creating a new file.** A window will pop up and ask you what you want to name it. Documents will often *default* to naming themselves *Doc1*.

Here's how to save a document:

1. Move your mouse to *File*, left-click, slide down to *Save*, left-click. Or, click on the *save icon.*

2. Notice the "Save In" box. This is the folder where your file will be saved. It often defaults to "My Documents".

3. To give your new document a name, click your mouse in the *File name* box. That will highlight where it says "Doc1".

4. With *Doc1* highlighted, type in the new name you want to give your document.

5. Left-click the *Save* button. Ta Da!

Save As

The next command down the File menu is *Save As*. *Save As* lets you save a document into another folder, or to save it in the same folder, with a different name. This is great if you decide you don't want to lose or change your original work.

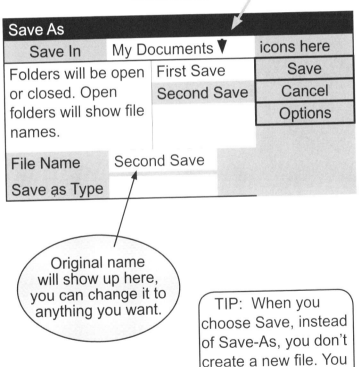

Click on this arrow and you will see other folders where you could save your document.

Save As		
Save In	My Documents ▼	icons here
Folders will be open or closed. Open folders will show file names.	First Save	Save
	Second Save	Cancel
		Options
File Name	Second Save	
Save as Type		

Original name will show up here, you can change it to anything you want.

TIP: When you choose Save, instead of Save-As, you don't create a new file. You will save (or update) the current document.

the File menu

Open a new document.

1. Open a blank page by either going through the file menu and left-click on *Open*, or by using the *New icon*.

Close a document

1. You can go through the File menu and left-click on *Close*, or left-click on the small x, below the *Exit X* in the top right- hand corner.
2. You can choose *to save or not to save* it!

Type and Save a little note!

1. Open a new blank document.
2. Type: Louise says computers can be fun!
3. Left-click on either *Save* in the File menu, or the *Save icon*.
4. Name this document *first save*.
5. Left-click on the Save button!
   Your document will stay open until you close it.

Save a document with another name

1. Open *first save*.
2. On the line below where you have typed *"Louise says computers can be fun,"* type:
   First you walk and then you run.
3. Through the File menu, left-click on *Save As*.
4. See *first save* is in the File name box? Highlight it and re-name the document *second save*.
5. Left-click on the Save button and you've done it!

the File menu

Save as HTML or Save as Webpage

This is a very handy tool if you want to put your document onto a web page on the internet. It will help you convert your regular typing into computer language (HTML) for the internet.

HTML is way beyond this book, but I will say this much: HTML is an acronym for Hyper-Text-Markup-Language. HTML is what you learn if you want to get into making web pages.

The Printing Features

Page Setup

Page Setup is used to tell your computer the size of paper you are using and to set the margins for your document.

Here's how:

1. **Move your mouse to** *File***, then down to** *Page Setup***. Left-click.**

A window will pop up, showing you your options.

2. Adjust margins, layout and anything else your heart desires. Click the "OK" button when you are done.

Ta Da!

the File menu

Print Preview

Print Preview is a GREAT feature found in most programs. It lets you see a preview of what your document will look like printed, on your screen!

Here's how:

1. Move your mouse to *File*, then down to *Print Preview*, left-click.

   You will see a miniaturized version of your work appear on your screen.

2. To return to your regular mode, click on the "Close" button located on the right side of the Preview menu bar.

the File menu

Print

The Print command sends your document to your printer! **Here's how:**

1. Have the document you want to print open
2. Move your mouse to *File*, then down to *Print*, left-click. Or, click on the *print icon!*

   A print window, something like the one below, will pop up.

4. Choose the options you want, page range, number of copies, etc.
5. Click the "OK" button and your document will be sent to your printer to print!

PRINT		
Printer		
Name	name you give your printer	Properties
Status	if your printer is busy or idle	
Type	type/brand of printer	
Where	what port its hooked into	
Comment	in case it has something to say?	

Print Range   Number of Copies [1]

All ☑

Page From [ ] To [ ]

Selection [ ]

Active Sheets [ ]

Preview		OK	Cancel

the File menu

Send to Mail Recipient   **}**   These will send
              Routing Recipient   your work to the
              Exchange Folder   internet & e-mail!

In the future, if you get into the habit of sending lots
of your documents directly out into cyberspace you
may use this feature. It is a shortcut, at least it is _after_
you have it configured to _your internet server and
e-mail address_. If and when you DO want to use this
feature, the program will walk you through setting it
up.

You may also see other programs here, if they are
installed in your computer, such as: A Fax Program or
Microsoft Power Point.

the File menu

Properties

Every time you open a document the *properties* of the document change. *Properties* are things like:

- the title of the document
- the date it was first created
- the date it was last *modified*
- the location it is in your computer
- the size of your document

So, if you ever want to know this very exciting stuff, (OK, maybe a little sarcasm there) click on Properties!

Exit

Exit is located at the bottom of the File Menu. Left-click on Exit and you will Exit and Close the program.

> **TIP:**
> **Remember, if you haven't already saved your work, you will be asked if you want to *save your document* before closing it.**

Bright Ideas

➢

➢

➢

➢

➢

➢

➢

the Edit menu

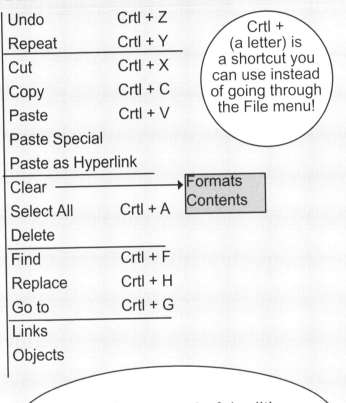

File **Edit** View Insert Format Tools Table Window Help

Undo	Crtl + Z
Repeat	Crtl + Y
Cut	Crtl + X
Copy	Crtl + C
Paste	Crtl + V
Paste Special	
Paste as Hyperlink	
Clear	→ Formats / Contents
Select All	Crtl + A
Delete	
Find	Crtl + F
Replace	Crtl + H
Go to	Crtl + G
Links	
Objects	

Crtl + (a letter) is a shortcut you can use instead of going through the File menu!

It's all these wonderful editing features that make computers fun!

51

the Edit menu

Undo and Repeat
Have you ever said, "I wish I could undo what I have done." Finally, your wish is granted!

It's really about that simple, give it a try. Remember, you can use the *backspace* or *delete* keys to erase.

Let's practice
Open a blank page and type some gobbledygoop, then change a bit. It doesn't matter if this is a saved document or not.

Here's how to use Undo and Repeat:

1. Move your mouse to Edit, left-click, then down to *Undo. Left-click*

Voila! You did it. But oh, maybe you would like to Undo that Undo (?)

2. Move your mouse back to Edit, then slide it down to Repeat. Left-click

> **Tip:**
> "Undo & Repeat" have a habit of changing their names! It depends on what you just did. For instance it will say *Undo Typing* if the last thing you did was *typing*, or *Undo Paste* if *pasting* was the last thing you did!

the Edit menu

TIP:
When you edit, you have to tell your computer what part of the document you want to change, by temporarily *highlighting* it.

Let's Practice how to highlight

Open Word and the *second save* document

1. Click your mouse at the beginning of the first line.
2. **Hold down** the left-click button and drag the cursor over the whole line. When done, release the button. It should look something like this:

Louise says computer can be fun

This is just on-screen highlighting and is temporary, it is only active until you tell your computer what you want to do with it. To remove highlighting, just move your mouse anywhere on the screen and click.

Tip
To hightlight an image or picture,
just click your mouse right over it!

the Edit menu

Cut

Basically, *cut* is an eraser. If you highlight text with your mouse, then left-click on *cut*, the text will be gone. Cut right out of the picture so to speak.

Copy and Paste

Copy and Paste go together. I think it is the editing feature I like the most. It's so fast and easy to do!

Let's practice! Open *second save.*

Here's how to copy and paste:

1. Highlight First you walk and then you run
2. Move your mouse to *Edit*; left-click and slide it down to *Copy*, left-click again.
3. Move your cursor to the end of the poem, you might need to hit the return key to get down to the next line, left-click.
4. You'll notice that the highlighting disappears.
5. Move your mouse back up to *Edit*; left-click and slide it down to *Paste*, left-click

Save your work!

the Edit menu

Copy and Paste with your mouse!

Here's how:

1. Highlight the text or picture you would like to copy.
2. **Right-click** your mouse to see its menu.
3. Slide the mouse up to Copy and left-click.

First part done.

4. Move the cursor to the beginning of where you would like your stuff copied to.
5. Right-click your mouse again to see new menu.
6. Slide it up to *Paste* and left-click.

Like *Undo and Repeat,* the menus on your mouse will change, depending on what you have just done. If you want, open up a document and try it yourself.

It's a pretty slick trick!

the Edit menu

Paste Special

You need to use *Paste Special* if you want to copy work from one <u>program</u> into a different one. I've used this feature a lot creating this book; all the little menus were created in *Microsoft Excel* and I used *Paste Special* to put them into *Word!*

When you use *Paste Special, Word* will treat your work like a picture or an image. Once you've pasted it, you won't be able to make any changes to it.

Paste as Hyperlink

Hyperlinks are what big companies use for those *personalized* letters you receive. When a form letter is typed up, a hyperlink is placed where something personal would be, such as your name. The hyperlink is linked to another data source in your computer, perhaps a list of customers. When using Hyperlinks with Word, your data source is usually in Excel.

How to hyperlink is beyond this book, but if this function is JUST what you need, at least now you know that your computer can do it!

the Edit menu

Clear

If you have a lot of material you would like erased, *Clear* is what you are looking for.

Nice and simple! AND, if you accidentally clear what you didn't want to clear, there's always undo.

Here's how to use Clear:

- Move your mouse to the beginning of what you want to erase.
- Highlight all of the material you want cleared.
- Move your mouse up to *Edit*, and slide it down to *Clear*, left-click.

Nice and simple! AND, if you accidentally clear what you didn't want to clear, there's always undo. Magic!

Select All

Select All does just exactly what the name suggests; it selects **all** of your document!

Click on *Select All* and the whole document you are working on will be highlighted!

Wow, it's a shortcut for your mouse!

the Edit menu

Find and Replace

Find and Replace work together. They are such a useful tool for correcting mistakes. For instance, maybe you have been referring to someone by the wrong name. *Really a bad thing in the Christmas letter...*

Want to Practice? Open second save.

Here's how to use Find and Replace:

1. Move your mouse to *Edit,* left-click. Slide down to *Find*, left-click.

   The *Find and Replace* window will pop up and ask you what you want to ***find.***

2. Type in the text you're looking for; look for *Louise.*
3. Left-click on the *Replace* button and you will see a place to type in your new word.
4. In the *replace text-box*, type *your own name.*
5. Click on *Replace* if you only need to change the word in one place, or click on *Replace All* if you want the correction to go throughout the document.
6. Left-click *Close,* to exit this window when you're done.

the Edit menu

Go to
You'll see *Go to* with *Find and Replace*. *Go to* works in a similar way.

Go to is great if you are looking for a specific something somewhere in a large document. It will *zoom* you directly to a certain page, or a specific heading, whatever. Open it up and have a look at the options it gives you!

Links and Objects
Links and Objects involve understanding source files, destination files, embedded objects... Complicated stuff beyond this book, but if one day you want it, it's here!

Bright Ideas

➢

➢

➢

➢

➢

➢

➢

the View menu

File Edit **View** Insert Format Tools Table Window Help

Normal
Print Layout
Toolbars
Header and Footer
Full Screen
Zoom

When you use the options in View, you only change the way you see your screen. View does **not** alter any of the documents actual formatting!

the View menu

Normal
This is what your *computer views as normal...* You won't see any page boundaries or pictures in this view. Some people find using this view makes it easier to edit work, myself, I prefer *Print Layout*.

Print Layout
Print Layout lets you view your document as it will be laid out on paper. In this view you'll see rulers on the top and side. The grayed-out areas on the rulers show you where the margins are set.

Toolbars
Inside *Toolbars* you will find the tools to dictate which *icons* show below the menu bar. You can control which icons you want showing through the *customize* button at the bottom of the Toolbars menu. A √ mark beside the option activates it. To turn it off, *uncheck* the box

Here is what a Toolbars menu might look like:

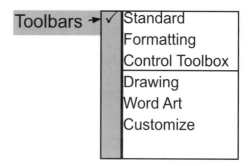

the View menu

Along the row of icons is a wonderful viewing option.

This *viewing percentage* % icon lets you increase or decrease the size of what you are seeing on your screen! It's a great thing if your eyesight isn't great *or* what you're looking at is *just too small*. Check it out!

Here's how:

1. Move your mouse to the % box beside the formatting icons, left-click on the down arrow.
2. Move your mouse down to the % you want, left-click!

> If you don't see the % option along the row of icons, look way over to the right side of the row; see a sideways double arrow? >>
> Left-click on that arrow to see other available icons!
>   Want to try it? Open *second save*.

Full Screen & Zoom
work in the same way.
        Click on them and see!

the Insert menu

Break
Page Numbers
Date/Time
Auto Text
Field
Symbol
Comment
Caption
Reference →
Picture →
Diagram
Text Box
File
Object
Bookmark
Hyperlink

Most of the Insert menu is self explanatory. The tools do a great job walking you through step-by-step.

From Clip Art
From File
From Camera
Auto Shapes
Word Art

This box, where this typing is, is called a Text Box. With a text box you can place special text or move pictures wherever you want within the main body of a document.

Insert Picture and Insert Text Box are the best of the best, but take a bit of practice. In the next few pages, I'll show you how to use them!

64

the Insert menu

Knowing how to use the tools **Insert Picture** and **Insert Text Box** can really up your overall enjoyment of any word processing program. Once you have them mastered, you will find tackling other options easier.

And after all, the purpose of this book is to make things easier!

Insert > Picture

With this tool you can put a picture that is stored in your computer, onto a document or letter. Left-click on *Picture,* and a menu like this one opens up:

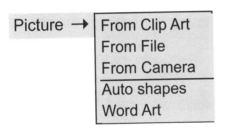

- Clip Art: This is a folder that has many different little pictures and drawings already in it.
- From File: If you have saved your own pictures in your computer, use this to find the file they are stored in.
- From Camera: If you have a digital camera, this will help you download pictures directly to a document.
- Auto Shapes & Word Art: These are tools that help you create cool looking graphics and writing.

the Insert menu

The easiest way to learn is by doing, sooo....
Let's practice inserting a picture.

Open up *second save* and we'll insert some clip art!
We'll add a couple more lines to your poem too!

Follow the steps on the next couple of pages...and
don't worry if you screw it up. After all, we all learn
best from mistakes!

> Louise says computers can be fun
> First you walk and then you run
> One, two, three, four
> Just a little, and then some more!

Depending on the age of the program you
are working with, the Clip Art window that
opens might look a little different. Most of
you will be using Windows XP, so I'll keep
to that here.
If you have a different system, don't
worry. You won't find it too hard to adjust
the directions to suit yourself!

the Insert menu

Insert > Picture > Clip Art

Here's how:

1. First, before you insert a picture, position the cursor on your document where you want the picture to be located.

2. From *Insert*, slide your mouse down to *Picture*, then over to *Clip Art*, left-click.

3. The *Clip Art* window will appear.

   - Every Clip Art graphic has a name and is filed away in a category. Search Text looks through all the categories for the name you type in this box, then shows the results.

4. In the *Search* Text box, type "running", or anything else you might like. You will see lots of pictures to choose from.

5. Double click on the picture you want and it will automatically appear on your document!

YIKES! Back in your original document, your picture is in the wrong spot and it's the wrong size.

No worries, it's easy to change!   Whew.

the Insert menu

Re-sizing your picture or graphic
Left-click your mouse on top of the picture and you
will see a perimeter of sorts appear around it. This
perimeter is then used to re-size the picture! You
won't see this box if you are not working with it.

**Move your mouse around the edge of the sizing
box and notice how the cursor changes to an
arrow.**

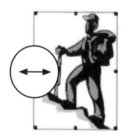

Here's how to re-size a graphic:

A straight arrow will re-size the picture. **HOLD the
left-click down over the arrow and move your
mouse.** The picture will re-size before your eyes.

The **+** shaped arrow moves your picture. Move your
mouse around the picture until you see it. **HOLD the
left click down over the arrows and move your
picture.** You will see the picture move around with
you. Let go of the left-click when you have it where
you want it!

the Insert menu

You might want to create a picture inside a picture or picture inside a text box or... *I could go on and on here. but you get the picture. Sorry, no pun intended.*

The point is that you will only be able to **change one object/graphic at a time**, *and* it may be difficult to activate just the picture or graphic you want. Don't give up though, just keep on movin' and clickin' and you'll do it!

Tip:
When you insert <u>a picture</u> or a <u>text box</u> a **"drawing canvas"** might automatically be created.

A drawing canvas lets you draw multiple shapes within a certain boundary - useful for things like designing a furniture plan. To get rid of the canvas, click you mouse down on the border of your text box or picture and just drag it off. The canvas will disappear.

If you want **to turn off this feature**, you can find it by clicking on:

Tools > Options > General

Under the "General" tab, look for and tick off, "Automatically create drawing canvas when inserting AutoShapes"

the Insert menu

Insert > Picture > From File

From File is what you use to access pictures that you have stored in your computer or on a CD.

Remember to move your cursor to where you want your picture to be.

Here's how:

1. Left-click the mouse on *Insert,* move down to *Pictures*, then over to *From File*, left-click.

    A window will pop up, similar to the one I show on the next page.

2. In the *Look in* box, search for and open the **folder** the picture is filed in.

3. Look for and highlight the name of the picture you want to insert.

4. Double-click on the file or click on *Insert.*

the Insert menu

Insert > Picture > From File

Click on this arrow to find
other folders, or other drives, in your
computer, like a disk or cd drive.

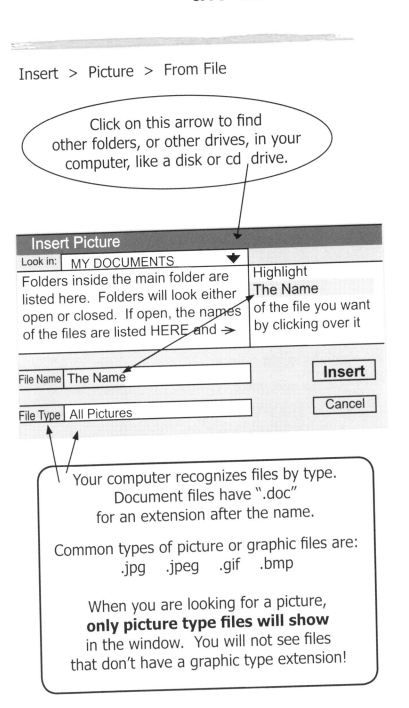

Insert Picture

Look in: MY DOCUMENTS ▼

Folders inside the main folder are
listed here. Folders will look either
open or closed. If open, the names
of the files are listed HERE and →

Highlight
The Name
of the file you want
by clicking over it

File Name | The Name

Insert

File Type | All Pictures

Cancel

Your computer recognizes files by type.
Document files have ".doc"
for an extension after the name.

Common types of picture or graphic files are:
.jpg   .jpeg   .gif   .bmp

When you are looking for a picture,
only picture type files will show
in the window. You will not see files
that don't have a graphic type extension!

the Insert menu

Insert > Text Box

If you ever want to place a note or even a picture somewhere special on your document with the help of a *Text Box,* you can!

Here's how:

1. Move your mouse up to *Insert,* then down to *Text Box,* left-click. Remember, a drawing canvas might appear.
2. Your mouse will turn into a **+** shape.
3. <u>Before you click down on your mouse</u> move the **+** to where you want your Text Box to be.
4. Once you have the **+** where you want it, **HOLD DOWN** the left-click and draw your text box.
5. When the text box is drawn, let go of your mouse.
6. Notice a cursor blinking inside the text box; this is where you can type.
7. When you're finished typing inside the text box, left-click your mouse anywhere outside the box and it's done!

the Insert menu

Text Box

Inserting pictures or text boxes is, like anything, easy once you get the hang of it. Here are a couple more tips that might make it easier.

Yikes, the text box is too small or too big!

Format a text box to:
- change the color of the line or even erase the line
- change how the writing borders up to the edges
- automatically adjust the size of the box to whatever you type into it

Here's how:
1. Move your mouse right over top of the line on the text box. **Left-click** to activate the box, then **right-click.**
2. In the menu that opened, slide your mouse to *Format* Text Box , **left-click.**
3. The *format text box* window will pop up, showing lots of options. Click around and have some fun!

> **TIP:**
> A text box, along with everything inside it, can be moved around your document. I often insert pictures inside a text box so I can move and place the picture
> anywhere I want it.

Bright Ideas

➢

➢

➢

➢

➢

➢

➢

the Format menu

File Edit View Insert	**Format** Tools Table Window Help

Font
Bullets
Borders and Shading
Columns
Paragraph
_____
Auto format
Style

Formatting a document, means to personalize the look of it. Here, you will find the tools to change the style of print (font) you're using, adjust the line spacing, create cool borders and so much more

Good news! If you don't like any changes or edits you make, remember thare is always Undo under Edit.

Oh my,
all the things you have learned!!!

the Format menu

Font
Font is where you set the style of print you want, as well as the color and any special effects.

If you want to change the font of a document <u>after it is done</u>, *or even just part of it*, you have to **highlight the work first.**

If you want to practice, open "second save"...

Here's how to change the font:

1. Move your mouse to *Format,* left-click and slide down to *Font,* left-click again.

A window will pop up that has tons of options!

2. Under each tab you'll see different choices, left-click over the choice of your dreams. You can even *scroll* down in each individual window for more choices!

See the preview window, it shows you what the font you are choosing looks like.

3. When you're done, left-click on the OK button to be returned to your document.

 ♀ FONTS CAN BE *FUN* 🚗 ♥

the Format menu

• **Bullets**
This dot is called a *bullet.* Click on Bullets and Numbering to find other styles of bullets. By using a *bullet* your work will automatically be indented, with a new bullet coming each time you hit *Enter*. To turn off the feature, hit Enter twice, or just click on *bullet* again. I find it easier to use the icon for this feature.

1. **Numbering**
Instead of a bullet, this will give you a numbered list. Try it. Open *second save* , highlight it, then left-click on *numbering.* Every line is now numbered! Click on the *number icon or undo* to undo it!

Borders and Shading
Have you ever seen paper at the stationary store with a beautiful border on it? Now you can make your own. Left-click into *Borders and Shading*, a window will pop up. *Of course!* Just choose the options you want and then click OK. Borders and Shading will apply to your WHOLE document, not just the wee bit that you can see!

Dear Mom,
Having a great day,
hope you are too.
Love Louise
    xoxoxoxoxo

the Format menu

Columns

Columns makes writing in newspaper style easy! You can modify material already written by highlighting it, or start right from scratch.

Here's how.
1. Move your mouse to Format and down to Columns, left-click.
   In the window that opens up, you will see a few styles to pick from.
2. Move your mouse over to the style you like, left-click.
3. Then click on the "OK" button.

Your document will automatically be formatted into typed columns.

> Be sure to adjust your Page Setup to be the same as the size of paper you are working with!

Paragraph

Inside *Paragraph* you will find the tools to adjust the **line spacing!** For instance, single spacing, (like this) or double spacing, which creates a blank line between lines.

the Format menu

Auto Format

*There have been more times than I would like
to admit when I have been so frustrated by my
computer changing what I am typing, apparently for
no reason except to drive me absolutely NUTS!
And then I discovered Auto Format...*

**Auto Format will automatically correct, or
change, whatever it sees as a mistake.**

For instance, it may see that you forgot to put a
capital in the beginning of your sentence, and change
it for you. Or, maybe you mistyped "to" as "ot," it
would correct it for you.

What you have to remember is that Auto Format is
only as smart as you tell it to be *(or as smart as some
programmer told it to be)!* So, you need to know how
to change *Auto Format* if you want to.

Here's how:

There are generally two ways to get to a window
that shows all the options in Auto Format:

- One is through this *Format* menu, to *Auto
  Format*, then click on *options*.

- The other is through the *Tools* menu, to the
  heading of *Auto Correct*.

the Format menu

Auto Format

In the Auto format window you will see plenty of options. A **√** mark beside an option activates it. To turn it off, *uncheck* the box.

This is also where spelling mistakes are set up to be automatically corrected. You may want to customize it for your own most common typos!

Here's how:

- In the Auto Correct window, type your common mistake in the *Replace* box. Maybe "rong"

- In the box titled *With*, type the correct version of it, "wrong."

- Click on the OK button, and you will have re-formatted Auto Format!

No worries, my computer will fix it for me!

the Format menu

Style

Style works a bit like *Auto Format*, but on a larger scale. With style you can access different templates. These can be for anything from a letter to a resume and much in between. *Style* certainly makes it easier for a regular Joe to look pretty darn slick!

Like Auto Format there are two ways to get to it!
Here's how:

1. Left-click through the *Format* menu, down to *Style*; here, you will see a small window with all the styles listed together on one page.

or

2. In the *File* menu, down to *New*, left-click. Through the File menu, you will see a sidebar appear with more options. Click on an option to see more styles.

Both of the *Style* windows do the same things, they just have a different way of showing it!

Basketball?
Anyone?

Bright Ideas

>

>

>

>

>

>

>

the Tools menu

File Edit View Insert Format	**Tools** Table Window Help
	Spelling and Grammar
	Language ⟶
	Word Count
	Speech
	Track Changes
	Protect document
	Letters and Mailings→
	Macro
	Templates and Add-ins
	Customize
	Options

I love the spell checker! It's like having your 5th grade teacher correcting your mistakes, as you make them! (Thanks Mrs. Currie)

The other options in Tools are just as useful, from asking *Word* to recognize different languages, to helping you with envelopes labels.

It's all here!

the Tools menu

Spelling and Grammar

The infamous *Spell Checker*! No longer do you have to worry about misspelled words. Spell checker scans your document and will point out any words it doesn't recognize. *Word* will try to tell you twice what it sees as a spelling mistake.

1. As soon as it sees an error, *Word* will draw a squiggly red line right under the word. This is only to draw your attention to it, *Word* will not automatically correct it.

2. Through *Tools* to *Spelling and Grammar.* You guessed it, *Word* can also check your grammar!

Spell check won't always be right, for instance my computer used to tell me Latremouille was a spelling mistake. Go figure! I had to *add* my name to its dictionary so it would recognize it as correct.

the Tools menu

Spelling and Grammar
Here's how:
1. Open your document.
2. Move your mouse to Tools, then down to Spelling and Grammar, left-click.

The *Spelling and Grammar* window will pop up.

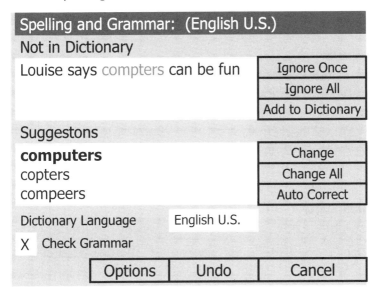

You will see your misspelled word highlighted in a box. Another box has suggested spellings. If you like the suggestion, highlight it and choose *Change*.

The buttons off to the right are plainly labeled:
- **Ignore**, if you DON'T want the word corrected.

- **Add to Dictionary**, if the word is spelled correctly but not in the system's dictionary.

- **Change**, if you DO want the word corrected.

the Tools menu

Word Count
Word Count is handy for school projects when the teacher asks for a "500 word essay." This tool will count the words for you. Curious? Highlight all of *second save* then left-click on *Word Count* to see how many words there are.

Speech
Talk about futuristic, with this tool turned on, Word can type what you talk! Now, if it was only as easy as that. Describing how to use *Speech* is a book in itself, so I'm not getting into it here. But if this is just what you need, now you know its here!

Language
Just like you or I might speak different languages, so can your computer. *Word* can even recognize mistakes that have been made in another language, if you tell it to! You will find a thesaurus here too!

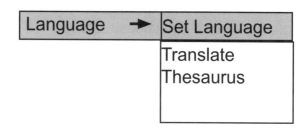

the Tools menu

Language

Here's how:

1. Move your mouse to *Tools* then down to *Languages*, left-click.
2. Slide your mouse over to the tool of your choice and left-click.
3. Follow the prompts in the window that pops up.

Try these tools with second save, you'll be amazed how easy they are!

In the *Set Language* window, notice the **Default button.** *If you click on it you will set* whatever language you have highlighted as the normal language for *Word.* Word first warns you and then it will ask you, if you are sure you want to change the default - Yes if you do, No if you don't! Don't be afraid!

If the language you need is not there, you may have to download and install it. Have a look in *Help* to find out more about downloading languages.

I'm also fond of the thesaurus. It's another tool that my grade 5 teacher insisted upon, although then the thesaurus was an actual book.

the Tools menu

Track Changes
If you are editing a document and would like to *Track* version 1, 2, 3 etc., or maybe you have more than one person working on it and would like to see who has done what; this will let you do just that.

Protect Document
If you want to lock a document, so no one else can make any changes to it, this is the option you want. Once you have opened the *Protect Document* window, it will ask you to set up a password, giving you -- and those you give the password to -- exclusive access to editing the work. This is really as easy as it sounds.

Letters and Mailing

Letters and Mailings➤	Mail Merge Wizard
	Show Mail Merge Toolbar
	Envelopes and Lables
	Letter Wizard

Within *Letters and Mailings* you will find a world of *wizards.* Wizards are step-by-step how-to programs that walk you through what you are doing.

It's just a wee bit beyond this book, but once you're ready, you can learn how to do it in *My Parents Second Computer and Internet Guide, Beyond the Basics!*

the Tools menu

Macro, Templates and Add-ins
These must be great for some people but I've never ever used them! So, they are beyond the scope of this book too!

Customize
It's within *Customize* that you can change and set up the icons that you see below the menu headings.

Options
Options opens a big window where you can set up more specific things, such as automatically saving your documents for you every few minutes or turning the *spell checker* off or on.

Here are the typical tab headings you will find in the *Options* window. When you click on a heading, its page will open up where you can tick on or tick off options!

View	General	Edit	Print	Save
Security	Spelling and Grammar		Track Changes	
User Information	Compatibility		File Locations	

The only thing that used to mess me up here, is when you click on a tab all the tabs seem to re-organize themselves. Recently, I discovered that it is just the *row* of what ever tab I clicked on moving to the front...
(Yep, it was a lightbulb moment for me!)

When you're on a tab/page, it's very straightforward.

Bright Ideas

the Table menu

File Edit View Insert Format Tools	**Table** Window Help
	Draw Table
	Insert Table
	Delete
	Merge Cells
	Split Cells
	Sort

Creating a table with Word is really easy! And, once you've made your table it's easy to edit or change it up.

You can use tables to create calendars, phone lists, organize items into a chart, you can even ask Word to alphabetize your table!

Let your imagination go WILD!

the Table menu

When you first click on the *Table* menu, you will notice that most of your options are grayed out. These *grayed-out* commands will come to life once you have created a table.

Working with tables means coming to terms with a few new words:

> **Cell** -- Each box in your table is called a *cell*
> **Row** -- Rows go side to side (across)
> **Column** -- Columns go up and down

Draw Table
Left-click on *Draw Table* and your mouse will turn into a little pencil icon. You can use this feature to draw a table from scratch, or even add lines to a current table. You will see these icons appear on your menu bar when you are using *draw table*. There's a pencil, eraser and a drop-down menu to choose different line styles.

Once you see the pencil icon, just move your mouse to where you want to create your table and hold the left-click down to draw. Really, that's it. Open up a blank page and try it, you'll see!

the Table menu

Insert Table

Word has included a lot of pre-formatted table styles. When you click on *Insert Table*, a window like this one will pop up.

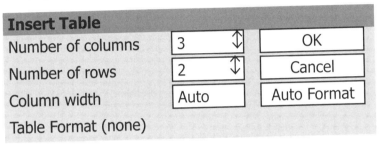

Insert Table		
Number of columns	3	OK
Number of rows	2	Cancel
Column width	Auto	Auto Format
Table Format (none)		

You can change the *number of columns* or *number of rows* by clicking into the window box and typing in a new number, or by using the little arrows.

The Column width set at "Auto" will evenly distribute the columns.

To find different styles of tables, click on "Auto Format" and another window will pop up, showing you lots of different choices!

When you are done, just click on the OK button to be returned to your document, table included!

> Remember,
> *If you don't like what you've done you can always Undo it!*

the Table menu

Start in this box and read through the table!

EACH BOX IS CALLED A *CELL*

Once	you've	made	your	table,
click	your	mouse	into	a
cell	and	type.	You	can
use	the	Tab	Key	to
jump	from	one	cell	to
another.	TOO	MUCH	FUN	!!!!!!!!!

Don't worry if you have created too many cells or not enough. Press the tab key in the last cell and a new row of cells will appear. Magic!

Here's how to delete rows or columns:

1. Highlight the cells you want to delete.
2. Move your mouse up to *Table,* then down to *Delete.*
3. Slide the mouse over your choice, left-click.

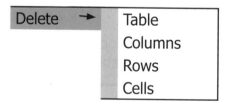

Now that you've got a table started, all the grayed out options are available to you! Most of them are self explanatory, and with just a little trial and error you <u>will</u> get the hang of them.

the Table menu

Merge Cells, Split Cell...

	Column 1	Column 2	Column 3	Column 4	Column 5
Row 1		Three columns merged into one!			
Row 2					
Row 3					

Three columns split into 6

To **merge cells** together, highlight them, move your mouse to *Merge Cells* and left-click.

To **split cells,** highlight them, move your mouse to *Split Cells* and left-click. You will be asked how many cells you want them split into.

Sort

Sort is such a cool, useful tool that I have to share it with you! You can use it to organize information, you put in your tables. Great for phone lists! **Here's how:**

1. Highlight the table, and all your information typed into it, by dragging your mouse over it.
2. Move your mouse up to Table, then down to Sort. Left-click.
3. A window will pop up giving you lots of options.

You will be able to sort columns, alphabetically or by numbers. You'll even be able to choose by *Ascending* (lowest to highest) or *Descending* (highest to lowest)!

the Window menu

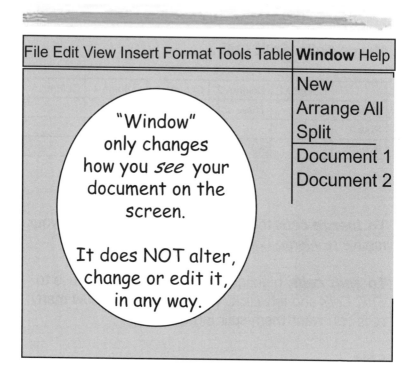

File Edit View Insert Format Tools Table	**Window** Help
"Window" only changes how you *see* your document on the screen. It does NOT alter, change or edit it, in any way.	New Arrange All Split Document 1 Document 2

Another shortcut! *Boy oh boy, Little Red Riding Hood had nothing on shortcuts compared to computer programs!* For the longest time I didn't come over to the Window menu. Now that I have found out how handy it is, I use it all the time.

You will find all documents you have *open* listed here. For easy access to them, left-click on Window, then down to the name of the document you want. Left click again and ZOOM! You're there!

the Help menu

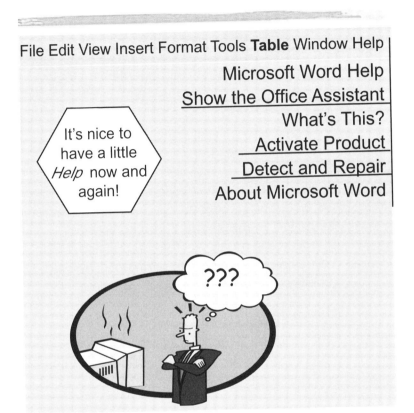

File Edit View Insert Format Tools **Table** Window Help

Microsoft Word Help

Show the Office Assistant

What's This?

Activate Product

Detect and Repair

About Microsoft Word

It's nice to have a little *Help* now and again!

???

Help will get you out of the worst log jam you come across. Though sometimes I find the explanation can be more complicated than the problem...

Left-click on *Microsoft Word Help* and the *Office Assistant* will pop up asking what you want.

the Help menu

Microsoft Word Help
Using the *office assistant* is a bit like playing show and tell in reverse.

Here's how it works:
1. In the space given to you, type in your question.
2. It will show you a bunch of topics that it thinks, fits with your question.
3. Left-click on the heading that suits your question the most.
4. Left-click on *Display* and *Word* will show you a step-by-step solution to your question.

Show the Office Assistant
Click on this and the *Office Assistant* will stay open. To close the Office Assistant, right-click your mouse over top of it and choose *Hide.*

What's This
Click on *What's This?* and you will see your mouse change to an arrow. Move this arrow to what you were wondering about and left-click again. A description of whatever you are pointing at will pop up.

Activate Product
The first time you use a *Microsoft* product, it will prompt you to register it, hence *activating* it. You can do this *on-line* if you are hooked up to the internet.

Detect and Repair

If *Word* just doesn't seem to be running right, using this tool might be all you need to do. It will do a quick self diagnostic and re-set the program to its original pre-programmed settings. Just left-click on *Detect and Repair* and follow the prompts.

About

When you are asked, "What program are you running?" or "What version are you running?" This is where you look.

That's it for the Menu!

Hang on, time to venture into the World Wide Web! WWW

Step 3, the Internet and Email, next!
Have fun.

Bright Ideas

Step 3

Step 3

Step 3 *the Internet & Email*

Not only will you find a wealth of information on the internet, but you will be able to get and receive your own personal electronic-mail (email)! Soon, you will find out the real reason so many people are on the net -- *because it's so easy to use!*

the Internet

E-mail

Needs & Wants

There are different ways to hook up to the internet, each technology offers something a little different. In Needs & Wants we'll cover the basic terminology and let you know what does what.

Your computer needs a few special parts to connect to the internet. What you *need* is determined by *how* you will hook up. *And,* how you will hook up is determined by what is available in your area *and* how fast you want your connection to be. *And* ...**when it comes to the internet, there is definitely a need for speed!**

Learning about the internet means learning some new words and terms. You don't really need to know this stuff, but a little knowledge makes it easier in the end!

For easy reference, you will see the **new words or terms in bold print;** their definitions are together at the end of each page or section.

Needs & Wants

Here are the basics on speed and equipment.

Modem

A **modem** is the piece of equipment you need to access the internet via phone lines. A modem can be inside your computer or be a separate external unit. That's just a matter of style, not power. A fast modem runs at 56,700 **bps**. With a modem, you can plug directly into your existing phone line. Know that if you use your phone line to access the internet, when you are *on-line,* your phone line is busy.

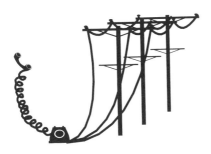

You can hook into the internet via any phone line. Your computer needs to be told the phone number of a **server** computer. You get this number, along with other information from an **internet service provider (ISP).**

A voice/fax/modem will enable your computer to access the internet, work as a fax machine and like a telephone.

Needs & Wants

Cable Modem

A *cable modem* is not really a "modem" but for simplicity, that's what they called it. It's the piece of equipment you need to access the internet via *TV cable*. This type of connection is very fast, running generally at 2**mbps**. Besides being fast, by using your TV Cable to access the internet, you are <u>not tying up your phone line</u>! With cable, your computer is always hooked into the internet and ready to go on-line.

Generally, the cable company will provide the *cable modem* when you hook up with them as your ISP.

DSL

A *Digital Subscriber Line* is a special dedicated type of phone line. This is a very very fast system, downloading as fast as 32**mbps**! With DSL, like cable, you are always hooked into the internet.

DSL is often referred to as *last mile technology*, because it must be within 3 kilometers (a mile and a bit) from a special switching station that is set up along the phone lines. This technology is offered by telephone companies where available.

Wireless Modem

A *wireless modem* actually uses the cell phone network. These days, you see airports and other public places offering this technology, it's even in private and motor homes! You should know that this technology offers very little security or privacy.

Needs & Wants

Definitions

Modem
Short for modulator-demodulator. It converts regular analog data that normally goes through your phone line to digital data for computer talk and vise-versa. A modem is the piece of equipment needed to access the internet via phone lines.

Bps
Bits per second. Bps refers to the speed of information being sent over the internet.
  56,700bps = fast   2,400bps = slow

Mbps
Mega bits per second. Mega means 1 million. In terms of digital bytes it's actually 2 to the 20th power or 1,048,576. (1 million is close enough though, don't you think!)

ISP
Internet Service Provider. This is the company that you pay for internet access and service.

Server
This is the Internet Service Provider's *computer*. A server acts as the middleman (machine) between you and the internet.

How to hook-up

Getting hooked up is really as simple as making a phone call and asking about availability and cost. Here's the scoop on the **who** and **how**, with **what** type of connection you might choose.

With a Modem
Most telephone companies offer internet service. They have a large computer that acts as a server, communicating between you and the rest of the internet. *Be aware that any company can offer you internet service, as long as they have the equipment.* ***Make sure the company you choose is reputable.***

A modem connects to a server with a telephone number that has been programmed into your computer. You will hear this referred to as *dial-up service*. It is important that your server's telephone number is LOCAL to you, or you will have long-distance charges every time you dial-on.

Each time you dial in, the server will then look for other settings in your computer confirming that you are a client of theirs, such as access and account codes, etc.
An Internet Service Provider (ISP) will either send a technician out to your home to configure all the settings for you, or offer telephone assistance when you set it up yourself.

How to hook-up

DSL

Digital Subscriber Lines are available through telephone companies. Currently DSL is more expensive than regular modem connections, and is only available in limited areas.
Call your local telephone company to see if it is available in your area.

The phone company that connects you should provide and install any extra equipment your computer might need, such as a special type of modem that can handle very high speeds. A technician will come to hook-up and configure the computer for you. Be sure to ask if this is included in the connection fees.

Wireless

Wireless is available through cellular networks, check with one near you to find out if it is available. For wireless service, you need to have a cellular phone service package. You will incur additional charges for any wireless internet use.

Be sure that the company you go with has wide enough coverage for your needs. Cell phone networks work on radio waves. Just like you can get out of range of a radio station, you can get out of range of a cellular network.

How to hook-up

Cable

Where the technology is available, this is provided through your cable TV company. Call your local company to see if it's in your neighborhood!

The cable company will send out a technician to install the extra wiring required, hook up the new cable modem, install any new equipment your computer might need and configure your system to work with their server.

> **TIP**
>
> With Cable, like DSL, you internet line is always active, but that does not mean you computer has to be **on-line**.
>
> You can work **off-line** as well.
>
> Think of it like your toaster... it's always plugged in and ready to go, but unless you push the button it is just sitting there!

How to hook up

Some things are common to all the hook-up methods. You should consider these:

The hook-up or installation fees. Some companies will offer free hook-up with a guarantee of your business for a term. Others will charge a fee. Be sure to ask what is included and shop around.

Free Email service. Most companies offer this, but you should confirm that yours will! You will want to know what is included and if there are *size restrictions* on files or mail you can send or receive.

SPAM. Another consideration is the company's policy on **spam** --internet junk mail. If you don't want it, make sure you can block it!

Companies charge for
internet service in a variety of ways.

Here are some examples:
* *Unlimited Use* for a set monthly fee, this might range from $20 to $60 or more per month - or more!

* *Hourly Use* for an hourly charge

* Some number of *"free" hours* per month, with *additional charges* for time used beyond those.

* For wireless, you can be *charged by the minute!*

Setting up for the Internet

Configuring your computer sounds intimidating. It's not. You simply follow along the step-by-step instructions that pop up on your screen, as the computer program's *set-up* and *execute* files walk you through an installation.

When you configure a program, you're telling it where to go and how to find information in your computer. The good news is that programs generally know where they belong and how to fit in.

A ***Server*** needs to be able to identify your computer, and your computer needs to be able to seek out your server. You configure your Email program to do just that!

This is the information your Internet Service Provider (ISP) will provide you with, to *configure* your system:

- Your server's name

- Your **password** and **user name**

- If you are using dial-up, your **server's phone number**

- **POP** or **IMAP** and **SMTP protocol** (don't you love acronyms!)

- Your **Server's type**

Setting up for the Internet

D e f i n i t i o n s

Protocol or "P"

You will see the word *protocol* often, or at least a "P" at the end of an acronym. Protocols have enabled the internet to work world wide. Protocols are rules that computers live and communicate by, making it possible for computers to work together.

Server Type

What type of protocol your server uses. If your server uses a POP protocol, your answer might look like this: pop.yourservername.com

Port

Ports are the outlets in the back of your CPU. Your Internet program will seek out and identify for you the port your internet cable is plugged into. No worries!

User Name

A User name can be assigned to you by your server, or you may be able to pick your own. It will often end up being your Email address name.

Name

Your real name, this will identify you with your Email name.

Setting up for the Internet

D e f i n i t i o n s

SMTP (Simple Mail Transfer Protocol)
The protocol used for sending Email.

POP (Post Office Protocol)
  or
IMAP (Internet Message Access Protocol)
Both of these are for retrieving Email messages, your server will use one format or the other.

In the window where you are asked for server information, your answers for sending and retrieving mail might look like this:

Sending mail
  • smtp.nameofyourserver.com

Retrieving mail
  • pop.nameofyourserver.com
          or
  • imap.nameofyourserver.com

You are telling your computer what type of protocol your server prefers. For retrieving Email POP is the most common, IMAP is a newer version that is a little faster.

TIP: Protocols are the Internet's "Rule of thumb"

Bright Ideas

It's a good idea to write down of some of the information your Internet Service Provider will give you.

Username_____

Password_____
Passwords should be confidential
Maybe, just write down a password "hint" here.

SMTP _____

POP_____

IMAP_____

ISP_____

ISP Help Phone #_____

Web browsers

A **Web Browser** is a program that lets you *surf the net* on the world wide web, (www)!

Two companies have an overwhelming share of the market for this, Microsoft and Mozilla. Their web browsers are called Microsoft Internet Explorer and Mozilla Firefox.

Most *browsers* are relatively simple to use and offer email platforms that allow you to send and receive personal email. Which browser you choose is really a question of preference, liking how they look and getting used to where things are.

All *browsers work with the internet*, in that they support the *common protocols* that let you surf the web and send Email anywhere.

- Explorer's email program is called *Outlook, or with Vista you might default to Windows Mail.*

- Firefox's email program is *Thunderbird.*

Browsing the Internet

Surfing the web.
Too cool dude!

Each type of web browser wants to look a little different from its competitor. You will even see different names for basically the same tools. The good news is that ALL the browsers have to work with the same *protocols,* so even though they may look different, they all do pretty much the same thing.

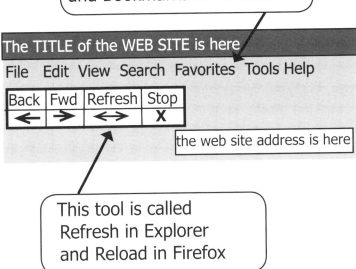

This tool is called Favorites in Explorer and Bookmarks in Firefox.

The TITLE of the WEB SITE is here

File   Edit   View   Search   Favorites   Tools Help

Back	Fwd	Refresh	Stop
←	→	↔	X

the web site address is here

This tool is called Refresh in Explorer and Reload in Firefox

Browsing the Internet

The whole web site address or web address is also known as the **Uniform Resource Locator (URL)**

There are three parts to a URL. The first part tells your server what type of protocol it uses. **http://** is the prefix you will see for most web sites. If you are downloading from a site or adding information to a site, you will see this prefix, **ftp://**

The second part of the address is called the **domain name**. People often only say this part of the address, omitting the prefix. That's okay because your server can often figure the prefix out for itself.

Domain names are generally all in lower case (no capital letters) and never ever have spaces in between words.

A typical web address (URL) might look like this:

http://www.nameofthesite.com

Browsing the Internet

The different parts of a web address are divided by periods, they are referred to as **dot**.

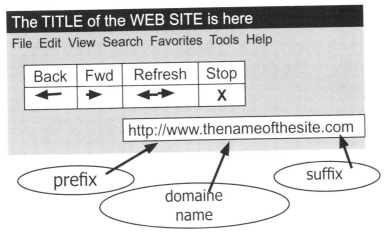

The *suffix* gives you an idea of
what type of web page it is.
Here are some examples:

.com Commercial Business

.ca Canada

.edu Educational Institution

.gov Government Agency

.mil Military

.net Network Organization

.org Organization (non-profit)

Browsing the Internet

A ***home page*** is like a cover to a book.
A small website might only have a home page.

When you look at a web address, the three parts in the beginning of the address are *Home.*

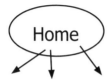

http://www.nameofthesite.com**/**index**/**orderform

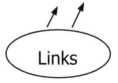

Slashes at the end of an address indicate **links**, or if you like, other pages within that web site.

Often you will see LOTS of slashes and links at the end of an address. The larger the site, the more links (pages within pages) there will be!

Searching the Internet

Looking for information on the internet has been made easy with *Search Engines*. You really don't have to know *how* they work to use them. But, knowing what they are looking for, will make searching easier.

D e f i n i t i o n s

Search Engines are dedicated servers with programs that send out *spiders* (also called web crawlers).

Spiders look for *keywords* that are imbedded in web pages.

Keywords are words that describe what's in a web site.
You often don't see keywords when you view a site. They are part of the *html* that is hidden on the viewing page because they are only meant to help search engines find the site.

HTML Hyper Text Markup Language is the computer language that most web sites are written in.

Searching the Internet

There are many *search engines*.

You will probably see a *search* button on your browser's menu that will be linked to one or more search engines. Some of the most popular and larger search engines are:

Google, Yahoo, AskJeeves and Mamma

There will be a window on the search engine's home page where you type in what you are looking for.

Searching the Internet

To practice, let's do a Google search.

Here's how:
  1. Open your browser and click your mouse in the box where you can type a web address; type:
  ## www.google.com

On Google's home page you will see a boxed-in window where you can type in your query.

  2. Type in the word ***vacation***, then click on Search.

A ton of results will show up. It could be thousands. To narrow down your search, search again, but be more specific. Maybe you want to holiday in Nova Scotia, Canada.

  3. Click back into the search box and type:
  ### *vacation Nova Scotia Canada*

Search engine *spiders* try to match up your words with web site *keywords*. They then will show you all the results they found. You can even be more specific! Maybe you are searching for a hotel?

  4. Click back into the search box and type:
  ### *vacation Nova Scotia Canada hotel*

Searching the Internet

See the pattern? The more *keywords* that you can think of, the better. Your search engine will do the work. Just click on the web site, from the resulting list, that you want to look at!

Tip:
If you want a search engine to search for **all the words** or *the phrase* instead of each individual word, **use "parentheses"**!

For example; if you type in *Nova Scotia*, you will get hits for the single word "Nova" too. Good enough if you want to learn about outer space, but if you plan on staying on earth...

With parentheses around "Nova Scotia", search engine spiders will only look for the words together.

Common threads

Browsers make it easy to get around the internet and a fast connection can make it fun.

Point, Click, Zoom!

Like the commands in *Microsoft Word* are common with other programs, different web browsers have common threads too.

If you use different browsers, you might see a different name on the tool you want. For instance;

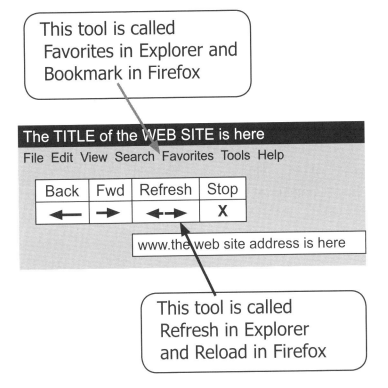

This tool is called Favorites in Explorer and Bookmark in Firefox

The TITLE of the WEB SITE is here

File Edit View Search Favorites Tools Help

Back	Fwd	Refresh	Stop
←	→	←→	X

www.the web site address is here

This tool is called Refresh in Explorer and Reload in Firefox

Common threads

You will find all the usual tools within File, Edit, View, etc., but the most commonly used tools on a web browser generally have an icon or button to click on.

The tools used the most are Back, Forward, Refresh Stop and Favorites. **Here's what they do:**

Back
Brings your browser back to the previous web page you were looking at.

Forward
Sends your browser forward again, if you went *back!*

Refresh or **Reload**
Reloads the current page you are looking at. Sometimes this is necessary if your screen seems frozen, or the web site is not loading properly.

Stop
You might end up at a site that is taking way too long to download, or maybe a bit of it has downloaded and you notice this is a site you do NOT want to see. It's nice to be able to stop things and try again.

Favorites or **Bookmarks**
When you find a web site you like, or a site that you will access often, this tool will give you point & click, quick access to it!

Common threads

Bookmarking favorite web sites

Favorites, file and catalogue web addresses for you. Once you *bookmark* a web site, you just have to go into this list and click on the site you want. Your browser will automatically take you right there.

You can even organize your favorite web sites into their own folders. Put a medical site into a folder named *Health*, or your favorite team into *Sports*.

If you don't file a web site into a folder, it will automatically be put at the bottom of the list you see.

Here's how:

First,
You must be on a web site to bookmark it.

1. Move your mouse to the menu bar and click on *Bookmark* or *Favorites*.

2. Some of the first options you may see on the bookmark list are: *Add to Favorites, Organize Favorites, Bookmark Page, File Bookmark*

3. Follow along with the prompt in the window that opens.

4. You will see a spot where you can name the web site you're marking. You are allowed to name it anything you like.

Bright Ideas

➢

➢

➢

➢

➢

➢

➢

electronic mail "e-mail"

E-mail is definitely not your typical snail mail! It is almost instantaneous, almost as fast as the telephone! Electronic mail is used to send letters, documents and files via the world wide web.

You can e-mail:

- **personal notes to friends**
- **digital pictures**
- **forms and reports**
- **movies and video clips**
- **songs...........and more!**

There are three parts to an email address

1. The name.

2. The "@" sign; *found above the number 2 on your keyboard, use your shift key to get to it.*

3. The server or domain name of where it is sent to.

A typical e-mail address might look like this:

yourname@yourserver.com

e-mail Programs

Way back in the book I mentioned about Operating Systems. Most Operating Systems come with their own version of an e-mail program. For instance:

Microsoft Vista - Windows Mail
Microsoft XP (and earlier!) - **Outlook Express**
Mozilla Firefox - Thunderbird email

Windows Mail is pretty much the same as Outlook Express. Just with a different name and an updated look!

Outlook Express and Windows Mail are both very user friendly e-mail programs.

Thunderbird email comes with full features and is also very user friendly.

Windows Mail and Outlook Express are abbreviated, smaller versions of the Microsoft Office e-mail program, <u>Outlook</u>.

Only very basic functions come with Windows Mail and Outlook Express.

With Microsoft Outlook, you can do anything that you can do in Word!

Getting an e-mail address

...with your Internet Service Provider

You should have email included with your internet service package. Give your ISP a call, and follow along with their instructions to set it up and get it going.

Before you call, think of an easy email name for yourself and a back-up name, if your first choice is taken already.

There are a few advantages to using the email included with your ISP, two of them are:

- There is rarely a size limit to the mail you are sending or receiving and if there is, it's pretty big! Pictures are large files.

- You do not get blasted with advertising banners, which is how most companies pay for their free email.

Getting an email address

Free email Accounts

Hotmail, Yahoo, AOL

These are just a few of the many servers out there that offer **free email** service. They make money by allowing space on their pages for advertising.

To set up your free email account, go to that server's home page and look for an email button to click on. Then answer the questions at the prompts and you've done it! Easy as pie!

Hotmail is offered by Microsoft, go to *msn.com* to sign up. For *yahoo* mail, go to *yahoo.com* and for *AOL (America on Line)* go to *aol.com*.

One of the biggest advantages to using this type of email account is that it is very easy to log-on and check your email from **any internet access port in the world!**

Sending & Receiving email

Here's a sample of typical email page headings in two different email programs. Same functions, different names!

Microsoft Outlook			
File Edit View Tools Actions Help			
New	Send/Receive	Reply	Forward

yourmail@netscape.com			
File Edit View Message Tools Help			
Compose	Get Msgs	Reply	Forward

You'll see larger buttons for the most used commands.

In different programs you might see different names on the headings, but essentially they will all DO the same things. For instance, here I've shown *New* and *Compose,* other programs might say *Create Mail*, *Write Mail*. The creative wording is endless!

On the next few pages we'll cover these common threads:

- Send/Receive, or Get Msgs	- Forward or Fwd
	- New Msg or Compose
- How to open email	- Attachments and Links
- Reply	- Delete or X
- Reply All	- Print

Sending & Receiving email

Send/Receive
When someone sends you email, it stays at your server until you ask for it.

The *Send/Receive* command asks the server to send your mail to your computer. This command can also be used to send mail that you have written.

How to open an email message
Newly received email will be filed directly to your *Inbox.*

You might have to look for the Inbox tab along the headings, click on it to open the Inbox folder. The Inbox folder will show a list of all your mail. The list will show the subject of the email, who it is from and the date it was sent.

New mail will be shown in **bold print**, read mail will be in regular print. Click on any item and you will highlight the line it is on. **Double-click** to open the email.

Sending & Receiving email

Reply

Reply is a great shortcut for replying to mail. Click on it and the window that pops up will already have the return address and the subject. It will include a copy of whatever they sent you, as well as have space for you to write in. *How cool IS this!*

Reply All

If you receive mail that was sent to more than one person and you would like to reply to everyone on its mailing list, this is just what you need. Click on this button and your reply will be sent to **everyone**.

Forward

If you have received an email that you would like to forward on to someone else, this is the button for you. When you receive forwarded mail you will see **fwd** in the subject line.

>When you create or receive forwarded email, bullets
>will show up at the beginning of each line; like what
>I show here. If you do not want these, then you
>should copy the text of the email and paste it into a
>new email.

Sending & Receiving email

New

Click on *New* to compose a new message. A new window will open up with space for you to fill in the recipient's address, the subject of the message and blank space for you to write your note.

A new message page might look like this:

< > Parenthese always surround an email address

Composition			
File Edit View Insert Format Options Tools Help			
Send	Address	Attach	
From:	your name and <email address>		
To:	recipient's name and <email address>		
Subject:	new puppy		

In this space, you can type your message.

Dear Mom,
We have a new puppy! I'll attach a picture soon.

Attachments and Links

Attachments and Links

Attaching a file or *adding a link* to your message is one of those little things that sounds very high tech and complicated. I suppose the actual logistics are, but from our end, things are very user friendly.

What can you attach?

You can attach any type of *file* to an email message. Generally, whatever you attach must be first saved into your computer. You should be aware that some servers are programmed not to receive attachments.

Here's how:

1. Start a new email. The options to *attach a file or link* are only available when you are composing new mail.

2. Left-click on Attach, Attachment or the icon for this feature (often a paper clip).

You can also click through the *File* or *Insert* menus, where you will see the command *Attach File*.

Continued on the next page...

Attachments and Links

Click on this arrow to find
other folders in your computer

Enter File to Attach	
Look in:	FOLDER NAME HERE ▼

| More folders and files are listed here. If a folder is open, the file names will be listed next... | Highlight The File you want by clicking over it! |

File Name	The File		Insert
Files of Type			Cancel

1. When you find the file you want to attach, click over it; it will be highlighted.
2. It will automatically go to the File Name box.
3. Left-click on Insert.
4. Zoom - back to the message you go, where you will see the name of the file you attached in the headings of your email!

If you decide not to attach anything, just click on the cancel button. You will go back to your email none the worse for wear!

Attachments and Links

When you click OK and go back to your composition page, you will see the name of the attached file in the headings. Here is a sample of a composition page with a file attached.

Composition			
File Edit View Insert Format Options Tools Help			
New	**Send/Receive**	**Address**	**Attach**
From:	your name and <email address>		
To:	recipient's name and <email address>		
Subject:	new puppy		
Attachments	picture of new puppy		
You can type your message here. Dear Mom, **Right-click over the attachment and choose "Open" to see the picture.**			

When your message is complete, all that's left to do is to left-click on *Send.*   *ZOOM, on its way!*

Want to practice? We'll attach *second save* to an email message and send it to yourself.

Yes, you can email yourself!

Attachments and Links

Practice

1. Open your email program and a new composition.
2. Address it to yourself.
3. In the **Subject** line type, **attach practice.**
4. Left-click on the button or icon for attachments.
5. Click on *Attach File* and the window to find the file will pop up. Remember, we saved *second save* in *My Documents*.
6. **Look-in**, My Documents.

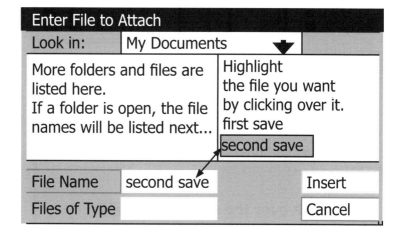

7. Click on *second save* and then *Insert*.

   That's it! *Zoom,* back on your composition page, below the subject line or in a side bar, you will see "Attachments" with *second save* in the window.

8. Click on Send to mail it to yourself!

Attachments and Links

Practice

Open your email and an attached file.

Open your email program and click on Send/Receive.

1. Click your mouse over the email you want to open, double-click! We named the practice letter *attach practice.*
2. Look for the space in the headings that has the name of your attached document, *second save.*
3. Move your mouse over the name, *second save* in this case. Double-click to open it.

There is another way to open an attachment, by using a **right-click!**

Important little trouble shooting facts:

* When you open an attachment, your computer first looks for what *type* of file it is. After it sees what type of file it is, it looks for a program in your system that opens that type of file. If your computer doesn't have the right type of program to open a file, it can't do the job.

* In our practice case, with second save.doc, your system will recognize it as a *Word* document and open the attachment with that program.

Attachments and Links

Some words of caution.

You just don't know what lurks inside attachments.

Sometimes when you try to open an attachment, a window will pop up and ask and offer:

- What program do you want to open the attachment with?
- A warning about viruses and opening files
- Asking if you want to open the file with the *default application* ?
- If you want to save the file?

These are all good questions! *What question isn't?*

If you don't know who or where your email came from, **don't open it**. **Delete it**. It might contain a virus, more on viruses coming up.

Attachments and Links

Links

When you attach a Link to a message you are simply giving your recipient a shortcut directly to a web site, or sometimes to another file. A file would have to be local to them or connected via the internet.

Here are a couple of ways to attach a link:

Outlook will automatically create a link on the composition page when you type a web site address, such as www.myparentsfirst.com

It's called automatically creating a hyper-link. By default, Outlook turns hyperlinks blue.

 Or...

In your composition window, look for the command ***Link*** *or* ***Attach Link***. You might see an icon, or you could find it within the File or Insert menus. **Left click on the command.**
A small window will pop up asking you two things:

1. What text you want your link to say, for example: "**check this out**"
2. What the actual address of the web site is, for example:
    "**http://www.reallygreatsite.com**"

Click OK to be returned to your composition page.

Attachments and Links

Links, continued

Meanwhile, back in your composition window...

In the body of your email you will see:
check this out

When the person receives the message and clicks on **check this out**, his browser will automatically kick in and go to
www.reallygreatwebsite.com!

TIP:
Be sure your link
has the right web address.
Go to the site yourself and right-click over the address to copy it.
You can then paste the address
in the link window!

Links are sooo cool!

Bright Ideas

➤

➤

➤

➤

➤

➤

➤

Computer Viruses

You've probably heard of computer viruses, nasty ones have even make the 6 o'clock news! It's important you are aware of them, and how to try and avoid them.

What is a computer virus?
Computer viruses are computer codes that are set up to replicate themselves.
In any computer program you will find *macros*. Macros are mini-programs within larger programs that do all the little jobs. Macros are a good thing.

We could say that computer viruses are macros written by the mad scientists of the computer world... macros gone bad!

Where are they?
Computer viruses are often hidden in attachments with email, but could even be in the main page of an email. They can also be in anything you are downloading from the internet. Yikes, are you scared yet?

How are they spread?
Viruses are always hidden, it is so easy to mistakenly send a virus to someone you are emailing. They are easy to get and easy to give.

Computer Viruses

Be careful when opening "Fwd" mail from someone you don't know. **To be safe, I would advise you to delete the e-mail without opening it.** And please, use restraint when doing mass mailings yourself.

Anti-Virus Software
An Anti-Virus program can scan any incoming or outgoing email, or downloaded programs, for viruses.

Good anti-virus software should be able to isolate a virus and maybe even help to repair damaged files.

There are many Anti-Virus software programs out there, but two of the more popular are:

The Shield Pro and *Norton Anti-Virus*.

Both of these software companies have free downloads of their programs to try them out!

<u>Be safe. Be sure you have Anti-Virus Software on your system, you need it!</u>

Deleting e-mail

Delete

Deleting email is VERY important! In your own home if you never threw anything away, cleaned up or took out the trash, it would soon be too crowded to move around in. It is just like that with your computer.

If you never deleted your mail, your folders would get so full, that your system would soon be bogged down with clutter.

To help things run smoothly, it's important to keep things cleaned up.

You should also delete *spam* or *junk email* without even opening it as a precaution against getting a computer virus!

You can delete email a couple of ways:

Here's how:

1. **To delete open mail**, you simply click on the Delete button.

2. **To delete unopened mail,** highlight the message and click on the Delete button, sending it directly to the trash!

Trash & Recycling

Taking out the Trash!
You have a *Trash Can* with your email program and a *Recycle Bin* on the main screen (Desktop) of your computer. **EMPTY them both regularly**.

Here's how:

1. Right-click over the Trash file or the Recycle bin.
2. Move your mouse to the "Empty" option and left-click.

If you delete something by accident and you *haven't yet* emptied the trash, don't panic! It's easy to get it back.

To Retrieve Trash in Email

Open the *Trash folder* by going through either the *File menu* or by clicking on its icon in the sidebar. You will see all the files that have been deleted. To send them back where they came from:

1. Highlight the file you want to retrieve and **right-click** to see a new right-click menu.

2. Select *Move to* or *Restore* and tell it where to go, left-click. *Zoom -- back it goes!*

Printing e-mail

Print
Left-click on *Print* and the message you have open, or highlighted, will be sent to your printer.

When you print an email, all the information on the top of it will be printed too. This includes the entire mailing list of who it was sent to, any carbon copy recipients, the date and the subject line.

If you only want to print out the message, then copy the message and paste it onto a blank page in **Notepad**. *Notepad* is a wee version of *Word* that is great for little notes like this! Left-click your way through this path to find it:

Start>Programs>Accessories>Notepad

Here's how to copy and print an email:

1. Highlight the body of the message you want to copy.
2. Move your mouse up to *Edit* and down to *Copy*, left-click.
3. Open Notepad and a new blank page.
4. Move your mouse to *Edit* and down to *Paste*, left-click.
5. To print message, left-click on *File,* then *Print* or just click on the printer icon!

Close Notepad without saving your document.

E-mail Address Book

Email Address Book

Part of an email program is the address book. Friends and addresses can be easily added, especially **if they send you an email first!**

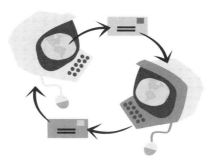

Here's how:

1. Open your received email.

2. **Right-click** your mouse in the headings, right over the sender's address.

3. Left-click on the option you want: add to contacts, add to address book, add contact, new entry, new card...

   Different email programs, different names and titles!

Some programs will leave it at that, but others will open an address book window. The window will show you the new entry and allow you to edit the information.

E-mail Address Book

You can also add someone new to your address book from scratch!

I have found that various email programs file the address book in different places. Click into your menu headings and find where they hid it in yours!

In Outlook, it is within the *Tools menu.*
In Netscape it is under the *Window menu.*

Here's how:

1. Look for the *address book* under one of the headings in your menu bar, left-click to open it.

2. Click on <u>Add</u> (*new contact, new card, new whatever... It depends on the program and what they wanted to call each new entry*).

3. A window will pop up for you to enter the address information.

4. When you're done, click OK!

Bright Ideas

➢

➢

➢

➢

➢

➢

➢

Index

Index

Index

Index

Index

I was simply writing notes to my parents on how to use their new computer. The notes grew and eventually turned into this easy guide. A fun, simple beginner book for my parents, your parent. and even YOU!

Computers can be fun and you should enjoy learning how to use one. So you won't find any techno-babble here, just plain, simple everyday language.

You'll also see that there are common threads between programs. Learn one program and swing into another! It's great!

This book is dedicated to my Dad, who lost his battle with lung cancer. With the purchase of this book you are helping to support cancer research - and a cure.

Thank you.

Louise Latremouille
Living, Loving, Learning...

Have a question or a comment
Please check out my web site, send me an emai
www.myparentsfirst.cor